W9-BEW-019

Strike Root

Strike Root

Anne Babson Carter

Anne Babson Carter

*For Jan —
with whom I have
the deepest bond —
to us !
and to life*

FOUR WAY BOOKS
Marshfield

Summer 1998

Copyright © 1998 Anne Babson Carter

No part of this book may be used or reproduced in any manner without written permission except in the case of brief quotations embodied in critical articles and reviews. Please direct all inquiries to: Editorial Office, Four Way Books, PO Box 607, Marshfield, MA 02050

Library of Congress Catalog Card Number: 97-61431

ISBN 1-884800-21-1

Cover art, watercolor: From "Dogtown Walk," Erma Wheeler

Cover and text design: The Creative Team

This book is manufactured in the United States of America and printed on acid-free paper.

Four Way Books is a division of Friends of Writers, Inc., a Vermont-based not-for-profit organization. Publication of this book was made possible through a generous grant from an anonymous foundation.

Acknowledgments

For their generous assistance with the editing and production of this book, the author wishes to thank Bob Brandwood, Gretchen Anne Carter, Steven Cohen M.D., Peter Herbert and Joan Hofmann.

The Christian Century: "Between Things"

The Nation: "Bells on Taiwan," "Domov," "A Killing Frost," "Sheep Sacrifice," "Greed in Potter's Field," "Cobb's Barns"

Paris Review: "Three Blocks from San Marco," "A Morning View of Bluehill Village"

Theology Today: "The Quarry," "Requiem for Street and Plain in Three Voices"

Western Humanities Review: "Three Russias in One April," "Miss Siegel's Boardinghouse"

"Cobb's Barns" was included in *The Poetry of Solitude: A Tribute To Edward Hopper*, Gail Levin, editor, (NYC: Universe, 1995).

"Miss Siegel's Boardinghouse" and "Three Russias in One April" were reprinted in *The Blair Review*.

"The Pink" was Runner-Up in the Lyric Poem category for the 1996 Poetry Society of America's 86th Annual Awards.

I wish to thank the Corporation of Yaddo for its support in February, 1995.

Notations

All quotations in the poem "Domov" are from *Letters To Olga* by Vaclav Havel, Henry Holt and Company, N.Y. 1983

The quotation on the epigraph page is from *Flannery O'Conner, The Habit of Being, Letters*, edited with an introduction by Sally Fitzgerald, Farrar Straus Giroux, N.Y. 1979.

All quotations in the poem "Domov" are from *Letters To Olga* by Vaclav Havel, Henry Holt and Company, N.Y. 1983

All quotations in the poem "Cobb's Barns" are from *Edward Hopper: The Art and the Artist*, edited by Gail Levin, a catalogue for the 1981 Hopper retrospective at the Whitney Museum of American Art.

For David Martin Carter

Somewhere St. Augustine says that the things of the world poured forth from God in a double way: intellectually into the minds of the angels and physically into the world of things.

Flannery O'Connor
The Habit of Being

Sow early peas. Plough flax grounds. Look well to your gardens; see to your roots of all kinds; turn up the ground that it may become light. Get out your winter dung.

Old Farmer's Almanac, 1793

Table of Contents

I.

II.

III.

IV.

I

strike: *vb*, to place....in a medium for growth and the
development of root

root: *n*, race, family or progenitor that is the source or
beginning of a group or line of descendents

The Saltbox

Clapboards fix a horizontal line.
They sustain what is true under a roof
that pitches to the ground in back. Cold stone-
work encircles the cellar, stacked well, while from the open
windows—it is now summer—a morning's
uncontrived light frames this house

in blue. Such a simple color, that, but not for a house,
knew the man who built it. He set its line
in white; believing a saltbox in the morning
should gleam, like milk, under a slanted roof;
like the chalk–white lighthouses we see open
to the seas. (Lighthouses too, are built on stone.)

To begin, he laid up dry the "bones," a center chimney stone;
then hewed with an ax the oak, to fit his unadorned house.
What evolved, O Rugged Structure, still stands—plainly open
to the families who have come. In its line
they find grace without clutter; from the roof
on its angle towards morning

a bluff strength worthy of generations of mornings.
All this implied the men who built them. What stone
metaphors they were, these laboring Yankees who lifted roofs
to cover their spare rectangular houses;
who let post and beam establish a line,
but who deviated from known parsimony only when opening

windows. (Yes, glass cut for open–
ings that colored the outside mornings
sometimes violet; or shot rippling lines

in amber to the afternoons, were goods of gold. Only stone
waiting in the fields near the house
was used as if it were the oak for the roof

that grew in the forests near the roof.)
How then did it happen—peculiar form? Once open
on a kitchen shelf, this uniquely American house
was modeled on an English box: in the morning
salt was dry (colonist too), inside his stone
and wood abode. A clapboard tells a simple line.

This house is mine—I the descendent of parallel lines
that openly assign New England's age; of times when stone
was piled for permanence, and roof planes met the morn.

Sheep Sacrifice

It is never a right morning
when we take the sheep from their rocks,
from the artemisia that is lacy
under a rising sun — a citron halo
that is always there no matter how early
I get up to wait for Anita's truck.
When the backdoor slams, shattering
a peace in the pasture, this day
until now without fault, begins.

The sheep don't care.
Only when I kneel against a fence post
after feeding them,
to run hard fists through wool
that never looks snowy on farms,
do they bother to look up
as though inquiring, "Are you still here?"
For by November sheep have learned trust.

I've fooled them with my grainy affection.
The path between shed and pen
is worn so clean even they see it,
and it will be there when next year's lambs
are dropped. As the seasons spiral,
each set seems more willing to be mine,
and I have come to hate this month
when heat dies, when the color passes,

and the grasses must be mown
before they drown in leaves.

Instead, our heads go up as a truck
shifts around the corner and my fingers,
kneading their cold, silk nostrils, shiver.
Now do they know why I stayed outside?
Why, in the same expectant air we breathe,
I vow never to repeat this ritual—why

at the intersection of two arteries
before a platform
with outgrown farmboys issuing orders
from clipboards marked "kill sheet,"
I turn away after giving them up.
Who can distinguish the faces of sheep
when names no longer matter.
In five minutes the stockades will be empty.

It is never nice to return home alone.
Above that empty enclosure fall's clouds race.
Twists of wool caught in the wires
like ribbons wound around children's fingers
to remind them, remind me it is I
who never remembers autumn's
inexorable return. I, for whom winter
requires a purpose

to repeat what spring promises,
I know that tonight, as I walk the dog
along the road, there will be no reason
to look up. No bleatings joining other summers
will follow our movements from side to side.
No shaggy blotches forever in tandem—
humped forms in high relief on a hillside—
will inform me it is suppertime.

Between Things

When earth and sky and things between
reach August, an excess so complete takes my land

that I back off from cutting daylilies
once divided by a Swedish grandmother,

to watch their cups pour gold
into a million humming bees,

their stalks like spires feed the sky,
and I imagine words these neon–throated trumpets

exchange with the cats
who lie coolly–hidden and unhurried nearby:

We, too, are free they billow
from their honey–suckled hollows — safe!

because her hand can't imitate our perfection
on a window sill; nor would she ever

sever our connection to a sky, to rocks,
to Veronica incana lapping at our feet like lakes.

Such is grace: to allow what fills sunlight
to occupy the ground.

Gathering History to Its Throat
to Be Repeated

I had meant to leave her there.
But five microcosmic tails initially alive
and therefore, dependent — twisted fiercely
like rubber bands to her equally tell-tale tail,

won't let me in the luminous night as moon,
strewing velvet over the old garden and its rocks,
casts just beams enough to shovel mother and litter

off the road. Look, marsupials may be ugly
with their prominent appendage ordered hairless
with scales in the rodent order, Deldelphidea,
but who's to say possums don't deserve lonicera —

the honeysuckle — they live among.
After all, tenacity counts for something
in the disheveled grey tunnels of our crumbling stone wall.

But, by the time I reach them they are deader than stones,
and their combined weights splay out so animatedly
across the open, steel spade, I am not steeled
from the summer I stepped down too quickly

and surprise! like blood! spurt between my five, bare toes.

Why are frogs so cold-blooded when their skins are warm
and their innards, viscous, palely slimy to the touch
while searching out even warmer grass?

This afternoon a boy mowed the lawn in circles.
He made silver waves on an ocean to echo:
what can't come back remains in us all;
reverberates down by the pond among the bullfrogs;

continues in their loose–stringed conversations
like the end bars of Beethoven
gathering history to its throat to be repeated.

Dog Star and Kingfisher Light

The entrance to morning is extraordinary.
      Swallows glint in the higher cold
      bickering before lunch.
      I observe the progress of orioles,
      and at noon a great blue heron sails in
      to reach the Connecticut pond.
      I have everything I want.

These are the canicular days. Pebbles lie beside the other,
      no one stone hogging more
      than its share of a day running out.
      Once these rocks made bruises
      like ripe plums on my soles.
      Now they strew points of quiet.
      I accept the sunlight between them.

Afternoons thin to green–gold. The phlox smell thickly like Persia.
      'Rosalinde' stirs among the leaves,
      'Starfire' lifts the shapes of trees,
      until by evening, too tall to remain
      upright, they fold, chains
      of claret mountains, drowning.
      Who will speak for halcyon and dog star?

At night everything changes. When light goes
      blood–red hemerocallis, bleeding,
      plead for more. Later others will die
      in the suffocating dark.
      Are we less without light?
      I am barren but the worn garden is still full
      of the rich matter of decayed life.

Solitude does not enter the city. It waits to be divided—
        unequally—among the hours.
        Insects cross a window sill,
        the odor to wood evaporates,
        and the only color left is black,
        except a blue sky of iris.
        Loneliness rises the way mists do above rivers.

Life is different in other places. People I know are elsewhere
        lunching outside the gates.
        They ride to work in taxis
        and unseat governments.
        On silvered streets of reedy magic,
        among airplanes, they do not see
        the kingfisher break its image.

A Silence Without Bees

Pulled by the sweet fern
I went out in the summer air
and the world waited.

I am a companion to rocks
that do not move
year after year,

quite unlike the fern
whose tangles are brief—
sable brushings against fall.

Nearby two goats wake their bells.

I am late
in returning to this air
which seems the same.

Once without thought
I walked to Cambridge Beach
wondering if the whole world

smelled like salt,
like a moveable blanket
in retreat from gulls.

Is an ocean a reliquary for cast–off bones?

Now in aimless moments
I pick weeds, lulled
by this wall of August

and a silence without bees.
Outside the cadence
of a month's mornings,

the dog, her nose pressed
against screened windows,
breathes in patience.

Weight the Bells

Hear the bells.
They echo notes of children's shadows.
My son the believer of clear morning eyes.
My son whose eyes are painted blue.
Sky–colored, the depth of water
They are sashes closed against the heat.
He slips among my thoughts.
My son without another thought
Than hear a door slam shut.
Who strikes the bells?
My son without a wife.
She dries her cloak of wild September grasses.
Moth–laden in this month
They are damp and smell of hay.
My son in solitude between his sisters.
They dance in unison in fine–seamed dresses
Different from his nature.
They tame the bells.
My son their father's child.
My son with strength enough
To burn a pigeon gold. No—
My son with the strength of half the world.
Cry the bells.
My son with smile of hesitance.
My son who hides behind a non–smile.
Who will someday give this smile away
But I will never see it.
The bells are choir–like
Sounding their echoes.
My son without a wife.
She lies waiting in the willows—singing.

My son with a future that includes a wife.
My son the color of summer sands
Which the wind will turn —
But not, they say, until November.
Peel the bells.
My son the descendent of hybridized trees.
My son with the bones he took from me.
My son whose jagged line of face
Is marked to be a map of Sweden.
Who will in this dry month
Of autumn ranges, disappear,
And to the world part–man, half–child,
No more mine, be.
The bells are yours, my son.
Cast your notes among their shadows.

A Turning Poem

Once a home to lullabies and humming;
to hallway curtains sighing when straining for a draft;
where spruce thrown straight had no time for rest,
and voices standing under front yard alders
allowed no sleep to overtake this place

of bent roads and winter tires; of incessant birds
feigning sleep on the rims of unbroken fields —
such keep dry, connected walls awake,
arouse the napping of wet fowl,
mar a landscape's doss.

All these are outside matters unaffected by my coming or going;
as are calendars, magnets, the clocks of kitchens
and sundials–anchored–to–afternoon–shadows, impervious.
Time to latch the door I painted Benton's Green one summer ago,
and turn away as a key turns in its keyhole.

II

strike: *vb*, to reach in the course of traveling

Bells on Taiwan

In the aromatic grasses
the water buffalo wakes. Alert,
this head of old knowledge, listens:
temple bells move the winds.
They play with the mountains
and ask about the sea.
They don't slumber, these leaping bells —
they blanket an island
where birds sweep like melodies,
and fields never finish their growing.

None of which startles the buffalo.
Born in patience to mud,
and bridled in charity to the trust
of small boys dozing on his back,
this two–horned ox of grace
who grazes over continents,
whose hooves plant rhythms
in the thigh–deep fields — this being
of metric stride can wait forever
in the long fragrant mornings
for the bells on Taiwan to be silent.

Three Russias in One April

1. The Moscow River

Let us collect the wood from the forest.
It is this spring, not last,
and impossible to remember
all we can forget.
So we gather everything,
even what isn't needed, stockpiling
the dead wood in neat spires
by the Moscow River —
as they did it
in the times of our grandfathers.
Only leave the ranunculus
and primulas to the sky.
Flowers die anyhow,
before they have anything to forget.

Yes, let us open the doors to our dachas
and breathe in the new air.
The logs of these family cottages
are parched, and the pedimented windows
need paint. Like the lacquered boxes
along the Arbat,
or a fanciful matryoshka doll,
these logs were once blue
and the mullions stained yellow —
to match the sap
running in the willows right now.
But so little remains
from our grandfathers. For instance:
who will tell us when to burn the fields off,

or how to begin a new life!

Already the forest is fertile,
smelling of mushroom spores,
and the endless birch we walk through
walking our dogs, drips catkins.
These trees are our histories.
They peel continuously;
into bands and chevrons
of black geometries — as though
they'd grown up much farther south, in Greece —
as though it were forgotten
there are no diamonds
outside Moscow
on the banks of a river in April.

Before the fresh–eyed girls
with pigtails down their backs
come home from school — how young they are,
these flaxen sisters without memories to store —
let us remember all we forgot,
the smallest detail of which
now appears oddly beautiful. Such as
how the grandfathers would brushpile
the kindling so carefully.
Then, how it would look
banked up. Who knows,
we may need it too,
to last out the cold
along the Moscow River.

2. Georgia at Four O'clock

Under the lee of a cobbled hill
a single bell chimes. What is it saying,
solitary bell, to the narrow street

where nothing is as old as its trees?
to the larch that shade fine–tuned acacia leaves?
to the interstices, the sycamores
dividing squared–off neighborhoods?
even to corners of youthful syringa
still growing? To whom is it calling?

the old houses filigreed by light?
the ones fingered by sun every afternoon
on their iron balconies? those same ones
once owned by princes of Persia — moguls
who hid their quiet fountains
within forbidden courtyards,
then entered them solely
through gates cast also of iron?

Is there meaning to this isolated bell
before its echo rises above
the artesian wells of this sulphuric city —
the warm and hot waters springing
from deep stone labyrinths caught
in the mists of its peoples — and reaches
the white spine rims overhanging
this tree–clad city, and is lost
to a higher, sweeter mountain air?
This is Georgia at shortly after 4 o'clock.

> Inside the people are talking about freedom.
> Around a long table they talk and talk
> about real things — about how
> there are those who are afraid to believe
> it is true, this freedom, it is so new;
> while others refuse to forget
> that to be a 'bridge' in Asia Minor
> means someone walks over you;
> a horse drops manure on you....

"Let us make use of the Shevardnadze factor,"
say these ministers with their dark eyes
and even darker eyebrows—
"that our new freedom will not stop
at the foot of Mt. Kazbek,
but become a belt of democracy
ringing these geographies
south of the Caucasus,
deep in Central Asia."

They hear the striking bell.
Within the yellow ministry house
they hear it pulling the people
to hope. Yes, drawn by a bell
into one union, here is proof
that afternoon will again climb
the winding hill, to settle yet again
against the frosted peaks guaranteeing
this tree–clad city. Outside

the sidewalks are cool to the touch.
While indoors, pansies the colors
of old Russia, that were cut
this morning and brought inside
from backyard gardens,
bloom on the long table
in deep glass bowls.
This is Georgia at shortly after 4 o'clock.

3. Snows of the Violets

In the snow they sell their violets, old women
who take their accustomed places
on low, hard benches,
to twist stems of earliest flowers
into nosegays devoid of scent,

it is that cold in the snow
on the day before Easter—

as though winter will last forever,
or God has forgotten Estonia at Easter,

but it makes no difference
to the weathered, old women
who occupy their stations
for hours on this cusp
of a grey, heaving sea, to wrap
their faint knots of hyacinths
in paper scraps more costly than the flowers—

as though bouquets aren't worth much
in Tallinn, or the Baltic isn't blue this far north,

none of which bothers
the gnarled–fingered, old women
who gather whether it's spring
or not, to offer narcissi
and limp–bunched anemones
at passersby who hardly stop,
in the unprotected square to look—

as though these women who have no boots
and wait through dusk in grown–old coats, know

where their violets go: sown forever
in tired plots of numb gardens
next to pounding seas—
the snows of these violets
were once seeds flung at the ground.
Now they promise children
who will root themselves

and thrive, in another country
than where their mothers and grandmothers

arise before dawn in the boreal air,
to offer wares of fragrant hopes
for 30 roubles (three cents,
that is), in exchange for violets
that, had it been warmer
on this day before Easter,
might have been perfume for Estonia—

as though spring derives from bright desires,
from seeds of flowers that were alive last December.

Three Blocks from San Marco

As evening lifted off the canals
and sounds we couldn't see through,
muffled as a vaporetto moving through water,
hung over our plates, over the soaked bread
and the meat from the kitchen,
over the red tile roofs
of this small fish restaurant

like an awning suspended,
we knew they were too magnificent
for husbandry—these three women
whose men were paying them absolute attention.
Clothed in linens as though
suited in pearls or glazes of eggshells
or chalk, they were smoking in voices

we couldn't hear; talking
in clouds so fixedly
that language danced
like feathers in air—like the blooms
off a Venetian Sumac tree—
until one of us spoke
and all humming stopped:

These women are swans. They curve,
long–necked; wearing assurance
that is porcelain white—without
eyebrows; only bone glides
ovate and gleaming.
Enjoying their nakedness they
might have called to Lohengrin.

In Venice with the children
how could I explain
that to remove something
and leave nothing
satisfies a craving.

Straight Through to Czechoslovakia

Driving east in the bower of an apple–green
returned spring
as rain wet everything quickly
and the fields, opening,
received their seed, I thought:
have I brought our daughter this far east
to learn there are places
to which she can't belong;
that once a mind isolates, a veil falls.
(It could be the rain. Or the night inside the night.)
My thinking kept returning

to all those who would like to be here.
The ones who once tied their espaliered pears
to every farm wall.
Those exiles who fled these cobblestones.
Do they still call to one another with light in their soul
every afternoon? Far from home,
over hills like shafts of bolting arrows,
our minds ranging (what is it that
changes inside barbed wire — the rain?),
we drove under the blessings of trees, regardless.

Prague Street Songs

In cities of languages
where the light
allotted to the old convents
ribbons itself into silence,
and the knurled trees
without their histories
are left to die,

people stop!
as school children pass,
hearing (they think)
the bright notes
of swallows
on the noon air.

Stilled (they could swear)
larks feint
on the reinless winds
and for a moment
no one says hush.
Freedom hovers in the streets.

Domov

This time the apples are on the trees,
yellow, and earth winters deeply;
hectares of wheat blow
in one direction like silk,
like meters of silk on tarnished stems,
and this time I am not afraid.
I have been reading Havel's letters
to his wife, Olga. What matters,
he wrote her, is how deep within you
lies the longing for meaning,

which I am able to understand
on this morning driving east
as autumn settles over Czechoslovakia.
Oak forests steep in gold.
A tangerine bathes
the country's reiterating stucco,
even small lanes lie open
to gilding (as do the telephone wires;
they shimmer with morning gilt).
Yet it is cold. Cold enough to snow,
and the light splinters our shadows
as we pass through villages of farm air.

Through a fence I see a woman
bent over her last green cabbages,
and in the next field a soldier
trains his dog. "The order of human work,"
Havel called it, doubtless remembering
how many people carry sacks of potatoes
at this time of year—reminded

how patient the laborers are,
the ones who repair
the polluted surfaces
of small churches by hand.

"You realize your 'other'
normal world....physically exists,"
he wrote her from inside
concrete walls (having learned to travel
rims of imagination to reach home);

words I feel on the orange air
as Krähe, those black crows from Russia
provide the earth
with fielding shadows of their forms.
Will they remember
what Russia is that this is not?
"The heavens make the stars
what they are," perceived Havel
from prison, which must be why
I'm not afraid on this morning
driving south into the infinite silence
of a Bohemian fall: freedom needs a curtain
to be brought to meaning.
Stirred by the cold, we watch
the oblivious birds wheel
like bands of airships in a rouge sky.

(In Czech, Domov expresses a sense of belonging greater
than its literal translation, "home.")

The Acacia

I forget the oats are blue in June, those meticulous notes
feathering now into crops of flowers. Yes, now

that the lilac have died in Herr Sturm's schoolyard,
and the vineyards grown heavier, I forget that air

can be this sweet: to coil in ancient motion
over meadows that somehow divide evenly each year,

the rape oil—beguiling forage; spring's tin yellow—
from the snow marguerite. More than 100 kilometers

south of Vienna, as acacia dust loams the side roads
and loops the steeply banked canals bisecting

Oberpullendorf from Langenthal, I never remember
how close we are to Hungary; that this countryside

no longer hides from the eyes of the sun;
or that blue doorways, lacking shadow, can't escape

fading. Just as I have forgotten the persistence
of each thing the hawk knows, as consciously now

she pulls to earth to nest among the acacia, squinting now
into the sun. I forget May would have been enough.

Region of the Acacia

But it is June and if we never come back
who will there be to remember two hamlets begun

three centuries ago. My sisters and I, we have mothers
who had no chance to forget. Separated by lineage,

custom, later continents at war, yet each planted a yard
when the acacia trees bloomed. Now one sister lifts her face

to some slight movement in the dulcet–ringed woods.
She is setting in her pots of pale celosia

on a ridge marked black by roses and a cast iron cross.
At daylight these forms read: Gebornen: 16.3.69.

Then silence. Who could bring herself to consent to Gestorben?
Instead only figures admit: 26.6.86.

My sister needs no dates to remember. She has been
to where I hope never to go. This I never forget

as I carry her back with me across grain–hued surfaces to America;
to a world that continues to grow in June;

to emit its acacia scent to the sable wings of hawks,
to the children of people now present, to those left behind:

to each planted within the contours of a ridge, a lane,
these bike paths out of stone encircling Burgenland.

Two Horses on a Beach

Two horses on a beach in Mexico. See them
out there, so long without riders or water.
Why aren't they galloping? Shouldn't it be?
Two horses bred for work — not play
by this air–driven sea of an indigo bay.

A man stands between the sorrel and half–breed.
How low their heads are lowered. (Would they disobey?)
We ask where they're from when not haltered
or tethered to ill–favor or sorrow
on hard–packed sand opposing water in the Yucatan.

The man's a bird in red bandeau, flowery vest,
hammered boots ablazing finely tooled silver.
The eyes too, radiate obsidian.
Yet each steed's back — the white one narrower
than the other, spotted one — is blanketed
in dank understatement. Is it customary

in Costa Maya not to return until late,
pesos filling your pockets? If so
where's the water? Where's their feeding bucket?
The birds brought morning hours ago
to this unbroken stretch of Mexico.

They wait in the wind (I can't look away),
side–ways to low sounds of waves being tender.
Each saddle is empty (should I stare elsewhere?),
but we are here to swim, not ride,
and they are as patient as the jaguars behind us
who stalk their preening jungle quarries

of Kailuum jays overhead. Nor does
the metronomic swaying of Quintana Roo's
palm fronds shade them when, after lunch,
off–shore prevailings rattle our palapas.
Beasts of burden, they endure
without apparent yearning, a sameness to Mexico.

Hours pass. So many since first light leaped
at the papaya trees. I keep watch and finally,
at siesta's end, a guest appears
to throw a sun–tanned leg over a swaybacked rump —
and they are off! Plodding at not even a trot,

the half–breed chained to his bridle,
the mounted one fettered to its reins.
How I wish they'd turn tail and get lost!
become Dragon arums — these two old nags
living off a beach's seasonal gold.

Nothing's in sight (where are the stables?),
only wind off the sea and oblong clouds
blessing this eternity. Much later, after a sun
had rayed down its furnace, we went in for supper
and left them to accept Mexico's forbearance.

The Patriot to New Haven

Snow lays bare the geometry of land
bringing roof planes into plain sight
and isolating cars vacated next to railroad tracks.
Leaving Boston, I stare down at unknown histories,
at shards of civilization no more elegant
than the nature samples we bisect:
what maple or sumac survive here, break
long before they achieve grace.

Yet these objects fit here above Providence
where more antennas than steeples rise up,
and The Pawtucket Waterworks operates
as one would expect — unceasingly
beside an ice–encrusted river,
its brick facade, unadorned.
Neighbors would be the first to tell you
people in factories don't need ornament.

Why else would so many of them
paint their own boxes lime green jello,
oblivious that some colors never enhance landscape.
More than geography separates these residents
from the current range of historically accurate paints
developed in Williamsburg.
If it weren't for snow
Rhode Island might be beige.

After Providence, bursts of tidal flats claim dominion.
White pines, knee–deep in water,
stand about like witches, talking.
Winter accentuates this cycle of bare bone days:

the getting up and the going home;
the work between. These people
north of Kingston might agree,
"Everyone has a choice about where to put
his imagination. Ours isn't in housepaints."

We don't stop at Westerly and suddenly
a bog so livid it flushes the skyline pink,
stains our eyes. In another season cranberries
will bleed from here profusely, like a spring tide.
Now clumps of boulders stonily pock
the high pastures at Stonington
and the only crosses left are telephone poles.
It is definitely Connecticut.
People don't live next to railroad tracks,

they reside in the serpentining hollows of a coast
and winter in other places. As a single osprey
soars above its boat–carcass kingdom,
we are across the Thames to New London,
city of clean yards and garaged cars.
Close by spills the Connecticut River's mouth,
home to picture–perfect towns wearing paints
brewed from dyes and named accordingly:
Bishop Grey, Bannister Blue, Vernon Yellow.

In a flash we bisect Madison
where Anna once boarded this same train— only north—
to Harvard, and I can look down on marshes
I've skirted in the rain. By now I know river names,
know where the winter–coated cows lie on Leete's Island.
I can be certain nothing as yet stirs on the Thimbles:
what brave trees flicking by like curtains!
In an instant our whistle announces New Haven.

I have skimmed over the destinies of others.

Is there proper knowledge here, or have I,
like a river cutting its new creek bed,
simply passed through a section of seaboard
as it held today—through its genealogies,
bird migratory routes, towns of severe beauty,
without altering a conscience. Nothing stands still.
The shoreline continues south into an afternoon.

III

root: *n,* an indigenous relationship or close and
sympathetic bond

We Are Composed of Others

When I am distracted by unkept promises
bearing the weight of grain sacks
before spring; when it is too soon
for June, for the lilies of the valley
in the shaded wood — and still so
for plums; when I am afraid of silence,
to be caught without words, or to dream
the dreams of rivers under snow
they are that quiet, while in the attic
two cats dance, to the tune La Vie
En Rose like raucous, eager lions
spinning dust to filtered diamonds;
when I am held by a fear of becoming
and can no longer believe
the legend of cranes we were told
in the Himalayas — the sacred one,
the one who returns each year to Bharatpur —

I remember we are composed of others,
of barns holding the breath of horses,
of lambs born to malted floors;
of one October when I knelt beside
an Emperor's wall and felt that sun
before it sank — deep, deep
within the chrysanthemum stone.
I remember we are pieced of sawdust,
of woven sheep, of late Februarys;
of the branches of some trees.
And we are forged by springtimes
that seep and seep through open windows,
as though in winter a shadow

will be cast by almost nothing —
by the tracings of a quill.
We are contrived of all else; of more;
of cats who by mid–afternoon
when it is fall, must search for hot stones.

He and I Are Pieces of Jensen's Boatyard

Around us   afternoon arrived as expected,
but now can't be stalled
in the hesitating light.
The tide too, was here,
until it turned
in one simultaneous motion,
as though one thing,
to leave the river

without acknowledging
that he and I
won't be back,
to wait beside
this bait–smocked sea,
slickered like seals
in our oil coats,
as one more day unfurls
into ribbons of pipe smoke .

At Low Tide   which force is stronger?
Do tides summon moments
away, the way
this black cormorant,
offending fisher–bird,
poaches? Or is water
sucked by time; altering
its course by so little

that these Yellow Legs,
flighty cousins picking dinner
from mud flats nearby,

do not see it go.
What is seen is only
half the evidence
as we sit hunched in the shank
of a golden afternoon.

Take these rays   which step in sequenced spasms
across our backs,
and we stretch — liking
the feel of a sun's dance
before it retreats to the hills
behind West Gloucester.
Too soon these traces
will disappear

and a breeze, cold
for shoulders narrower
now than mine, will blow.
What is imperceptible
becomes the events
we can count on —
those hidden clocks
that release a deep.

Invisibly   whether anyone watches,
a perpetual calendar
marks the high
and low tables
of these watering places,
reduplicating
the unconcerns
of a wavering afternoon.

As the river lets go   he no longer looks back,
glad (I imagine),
for one less day

to get out of bed for.
I do not urge him
to join the jest around us:
fishing—the act of—is enough.
He has earned silence.

I count the time between trains
paused overhead
on their tracks to Boston,
and hide my hands
to resist steadying his hands.
The occasional fish slaps our palms,
and the day just slides away,
an ever–deepening channel.

Time is dividing: there is what is left
and what is left behind.
I pretend evening doesn't exist,
and that he and I
will fish again for smelt
on October first
when it is 70 degrees
and warm in the sun.

Breathing delusion
in the salt air,
I pretend we are pieces
of a boatyard
caught naturally
in its ebb and flow,
and that waiting discharges
illusions of eternity.

Ipsissima Verba

I would see her facing east
without a face—cloth–coated figure
caught to a baby carriage on a park bench
next to a water–way
where that barrel–gaited course pounds
under a bridge and out to sea.

Throughout the worn–out afternoons
of that very winter, we never met.
She was told I expect, to remain outside;
anonymous until each last light
left each indifferent sky;
until the bridge lost its lines.

If she did realize my shadow
we never admitted its existence.
I had a history to return to,
while she had been told to wait
until all trout–spotted clouds departed
and the liquid days dissolved.

Once I saw her swallow from a bottle
that I knew must be Absinthe. What else
heats up hours until they glitter grainily;
until a lamplight allows, yes—
time to go home. (This is no place
for laughing. Who rejoices here?)

If she ever knew how tulips force spring
it would have been before, in Ireland.
Such things happened far away

and cannot explain the Hell
of sleet slashing storm windows;
nor the sounds of bare maple trees.

And so it continued, seriatim, until the morning
I read of a Nanny who threw a baby
into the East River where that tributary
flows irretrievably under the Queensboro Bridge.
The next day her bench was empty
and it was colder than a language without children.

One Habitation

an accurate naming of the things of God
Flannery O'Connor

What kind of person was she that it could be said
(years after she died):
the only unnecessary things in Idie's life
were her roses, hedges of them
lining a driveway
like pages of history
rose–watering a thoroughfare.

Cherokee, Prosperity, Penelope. The White Rose of York,
    O! brave talisman of glory.
The apothecary's source, *Red Rose of Lancaster.*
Did she love them more than God —
her *Honorable Lady Lindsay,*
La Reine Victoria, and the rose so like a butterfly,
r. chinensis mutabilis.

Her grandson did not say when her husband died
to leave her alone
in the frame house on Elm Street.
Nor do we know if all her books were borrowed,
or if she read them at night
before turning off the light
(to dream of roses?),
a cat curled there
through the hoarfrost winters
of Indiana, PA.

Bracts of trusses at every stage of growth.
Garnet stamens, edged sepals,

rolled petals swelling to scalloped, blowsy, tissued cups
limned by the old aromas of raspberry, tea, citrus, spice.
How wrinkled a leathery foliage grows when fringed
dark like deep woods.

It never was clear in what years her children grew up
to move away from that house that soon peeled.
Who knew if the seams of her stockings
were straight, or if she wore hats to church?
Did she frequent the same pew?
Instead he said,
she loved those roses wildly.

Gallicas, ramblers, autumn damasks.
A bulging Wichuriana revealing its quartered, giant saucers.
What about the "one without a peer," *Madame Hardy*,
niveous virgin bearing the name of the plantsman's wife
who bred her in Paris for Josephine at Malmaison.

Wasting nothing on choice or other lesser loyalties;
willingly imprisoned: a possessor
as well as possessed, and eager
to be pricked by winter's kill
at each returning spring
(at last a toxin to equal intoxication) —

think of that joy!
the unequivocation that allowed
no more gardens
than there are corners to the wind....

Gruss an Aachen, Sir Thomas Lipton. How did she choose
twice–sweetened *Shailer's White Moss*? What place had *Hansa*,
the rugged rugosa, tough as nails, in this bed of enchantment?
Is it possible to love a thing more than God?

....only roses filling an allée
until they too, rose up
and suffused her mind
(drowning all previous longings),
and she found excuses each day
to walk her pavement in astonishment:

they were hers! these cabbages and albas,
climbers and polyanthas,
mosses and perpetuals—hers. To her
they called (even in winter),
their flagon–shaped hips arching for more.

Madder, white satin, a copper fading to topaz.
Cherry pinks and lilac pinks, a crimson shot with gold.
Cutting their colors on late shade–drawn afternoons
who else but she inhaled their scent
of bee–winged, honeysuckled clover.

To have loved a hedge of roses more
than lack or sacrifice;
to be able to imagine your hedgerow a moor
free of all but rapture;
to have loved something so much you are that thing—
isn't that epitaph enough?

Unchanged *Rosa Spinosissima*, the 'scotch rose' true to species,
casting its fragrant apples to a northern hemisphere
through thousands of years.
Of the wild forms the first to bloom.
Felicia, La France, Ballerina spilling Hydrangea–like beauty.
Might unrestraint explain the persistence of God?

Birdman at the River at Sixty–Third

He calls into being things which don't exist,
this birdman of the river who lives freely among
the gulls he conducts on countless, brilliant mornings.
And later too, in the planetary nights,
when the river is soft and issues laments
which run from his sorrow, I have seen him
gather them to him—this Host! to Harmony!
to feed his flights of incoming cloud seeders,
mercy. (Plenty in exchange for Rhapsody.)
And when he conducts all aimlessness departs.

But what if I stopped? Would I hear it too—
so much music in the silence out there.
I am haunted by this universe of his, this foam
of ethereal feathers without corners.
And I believe the details of their melodies
consort with the airs as he calls into being
things which aren't there, at least to our ears.
Is music the ellipsis between us—we
who don't hear what shouldn't be. By degrees
I have asked, but never To Him: did you once

act out a life then discard it, the way one does sleep,
biographies, the fine prints of leopards
or the lamentations of former birds? Who knows
the origins of blue lights in the subway at night?
And what of constellations: are they pure in sound
but polyphonic in form? Tell me: did you never gaze
at girls in church—mute, before a sermon;
then walk barefoot just because the grass was there,
to later lie down at noon to rest

in the Iowa heat of an unmown cornfield? Though

      once, mind you, we did meet.
      It was April, a soft, green morning
      in Washington Square, and I,
      whiling away an hour
      until the stores opened,
      happened to glance up as he — well,
      for HIS reasons he had left our river
      and his harmonics — and we met!
      Face to face so unexpectedly
      we said, "Hello!" just as though
      we'd already been formally introduced,
      or were normal neighbors
      nodding out of recognition
      but certainly not affection,
      thank you....and I remember
      the momentary quirkiness of it all,
      for on our river he is never guided
      by etiquette. Nor would he ever
      tell me an earth secret. Such as:
      what is clearer than this same light
      coming up now, over Hirosaki,
      the soil's home of cherry trees?

Yes, who has lost touch with dreams? Do nothing but ideas
stand between us? I am afraid to stop,
to engage the salvation of a man unloosed
to a firmament — flinging out his fantasias
under a bridge, unpinioned; except
by the utmost parts of the sea. Yet I see,
that as he downbeats across our solstice
they have his divine attention: Laughing, Herring,
Ring–Billed gulls who lavish him with lullabies;

who are his square–tailed consorts; who lift

without plunging into knowing too soon.
(How they kite like kites, planing!)
Until I concur: in every life there is a way
to paradise, and I am called to wake among things
which are, but have no meaning. So behold!
Avian Maestro of the descant — Kapellmeister.
Stamp out your hornpipes! Unfettered by governments,
legends, or the sequence of conscience.
Meter them to a river crescendoing.

The Quarry

God sleeps in the stone
dreams in the flower
wakes in the man.
                    Goethe

"I've learned," you said,
"what happens rests in a man's eyes."
We were walking in silence
above the quarries,
single file as we always have,
when you began to talk about courage
(I call it that),
to decide: whether a man suffers,

matters. Coarse bracken and sweet fern,
unchanged since childhood,
curled at our feet
as we moved towards summer's end,
and you told me about a patient
in whom you found no hope —
until his eyes,
following your hands, understood,

and reached for those plains
where angels must live.
"Morphine is quick," you said,
and your voice, drifting over my head,
carried notes I'd heard before:
clear about purpose; as though in mercy
there is a purity
that exceeds pride, certainly regret.

Before us lay the quarries.
They were finished and filled with water.
In August's flinty light
I thought,
what do sick people see
behind those masks doctors wear?
Is compassion visible
under glove–like skin,
a green gauze gown? For a time,

on that open ground above Annisquam's coast,
a quiet, ancient as siblings
stretched between us,
and I thought,
in that other world where everyone is afraid,
where chairs are metal
and hard truths wait down long corridors—
where most flowers aren't brought
from gardens—would I know you?
There, where to think
about the outside, or to own anything;
to be soft or kiss
or let tears lift a man's body
(how easily it lifts
when it weighs the stones
of ten stones), are not allowed—

would I know the hands and eyes
I follow now
high up here,
closer to clouds it seems
than the abandoned pits below.
Where does courage come from?
Is it given out when least expected,
to be received unknowingly?

The seasons were parting.
Immovable stones led us on.
"Yes," you said, "it is awful the distance
some must travel to die
because we revere law
more than pain. I think
pain weighs more." Up ahead
our car waited beside an old road

once cut decisively for draft horses.
Now they too, were lost
to the sweet fern air,
and I thought,
had that day been a day like today
with seas high and the grasses dry before noon?
Did the world throb with insects
and the still, indiscernible water

have no bottom? "What happens rests
in a man's eyes,"
and your own
as you spoke
were the colors of sun–lasered seas.
"A doctor has only wisdom.
He isn't taught miracles."
And then I knew:

what else is courage
if not trust
where human needs lie deepest.
Our way among steps
carved a century ago
had been retraced. Soon autumn rains
would begin cooling this place
of waist–high weeds.

Miss Siegel's Boardinghouse

This town is where the Ottaquechee River,
falling from a glacier in the aquagreen
mountains, begins its descent
to another river's mouth. We are told horses
once sighed nervously here, before they drank.
Now birds take advantage of everything.

On this night the trees were preparing for rain.
We could hear them through the panes
of our second–floor bedroom, as though a tree
if hitched to wind, might flow through glass.
On this particular night Miss Siegel had been asleep.
Inside the cast of a bare light bulb,

dozing in a chair as misshapen as she,
we found her waiting through the spun–out night
for boarders booked by the Vermont Tourist
Association. But we knew at once
she had not always done this: wait up late
for strangers in the high–ceilinged silence

of a front hall lacking amenities.
Photographs said so. In cheap, black frames
from Woolworth's, tacked to paper strewn
with sallow roses, lives hung that told us how
she had once sat astride a thoroughbred
given her by her father; then, matching

her gait to his, they had ridden out
into the flame–filled afternoons, to return
in time for tea. "We always rode together,"

she said. "It was he who planted the maples
you see, winding up the hill" —fiery maples
we saw outside the French doors

of this gabled house; maples now
as entrenched as alluvial fans
on the Ottaquechee River floor.
"He taught me how to ride," she said.
"We always took the ribbons at the fairs
across the state," and her wheezing, splayed—out form

as we followed her up the long, banistered
stairwell, belied photographs that told us how
she had once sat beside her father,
slender figure in a skirted habit,
both of them solemn, in that moment
before they turned their mounts to canter off

into a crisp and blatant afternoon—quickly,
before a sun could drop
and leave a river bereft of its image.
"We rode even in the rain," she said.
"My father believed in it and the horses
needed it," and as she spoke we heard

the heavy geese—hollow over the cornices
and eaves of this late—Victorian manor home;
their calls transitory in the inky night
over the arched doorways, the chimney caps,
even over the outdoor furniture painted
dark as ungreenable black—like the firs;

New England's green; until their trumpets,
spiraling in the drafts of a river
moving downstream, died in the distance
of November's first silence. All this happened

long ago. On certain fall nights
I lie awake, wondering: had she, just once,

run out of the house and into summer's
braided sunlight without bothering to look back;
single–minded in her haste to reach a stable
where a horse stood waiting — waiting
in the shadows of an open barn door;
saddled and cooled in the latticed shade

of a double door flung wide. Sometimes
at sunset, as winds, fishtailing, release smoke
into dapple–grey autumn, I wonder:
did she at least once, ride unrestrained
on the brink of a future, letting go
the reins, letting go her pigtail,

letting the thoroughbred have its gait?
Until later, emerging from recesses
deep as cathedrals, did she crown a hill
in command of the Ottaquechee where that river,
dropping abruptly from a remote headwater,
curves excruciatingly?

As each new fall arrives, I think: where are
the thoroughbreds now? Who feels their strengths;
invests in their traditions? Does anyone inquire
if the stable doors lie open, still?
Is the air cool? Are the stalls that line the walls
empty, still? What horse may carry more

than its share of a swaybacked weight?
Who prunes the maples eagerly in the spring?
What does one ever know? Is there reason
for imagination, for midnight;
for this constant longing of what is to come?

Is it possible horses still drink

from the detrited banks of the Ottaquechee River:
bird–stained, hoof–imprinted, tracked by bears,
where this middle course turns from its source —
a spring named Montpelier Green.
All this happened before. Tonight
we are strangers who arrive to view the foliage.

Ignorant of the knowledge that equus requires,
we follow the uneven breathing
of a solitary figure to our second–floor room.
Along the way, thumbtacked
to yellowed, cabbage roses, a young woman
leans against the flank of a horse as it drinks

from an eddying river. Her face is turned up
to what must be the sun. We see no photographers.
Outside the trees are preparing for rain.
We hear them beyond the steep slate roof.
Night will soon isolate Miss Siegel's Boardinghouse
from the Ottaquechee River bending to fall

from where ridges form landscapes.
At this point in the system the channel
is unnavigable: marked in geodetic surveys
as too tight to turn the turbines
of an electric generator. Only south,
after the confluence of many rivers,

will it become part of a basin
that supports boats, a boatyard, a lighthouse — yes
even a spanning bridge over the Connecticut.
To a one these courses will remain magnets
for geese, for leaves, for a thoroughbred.
The river as Miss Siegel knows it — slicking

by her now full–grown sugar maples
towering over the woods by Woodstock —
has formed a wide flood plain offering
not enough footing for horses to stand in,
withers–deep in, to drink from, heads bent
and slathered whitely with fatigue, thirstily.

Requiem for Street and Plain in Three Voices

Dies Irae

In an hour this day will be over. During it,
the barest breath in the seventh month
in ordinary time, a child owning
20 summers and equal winters, died,
to separate from life as we know it.
Requiem aeternam. Done eis Domine.

Some days later, with so many of us
having to spill out onto a July pavement
slick with rain, a eucharistic mass
for the dead was said, but without music.
We were not allowed to sing
to raise our souls

off the chilled, marbled flooring.
Our clod–like feet remained fast
to that Greek Orthodox sanctuary—
we were as present as she
inside that black metal box
shut tight like a tomb.

Did they think we might crush her
with our prying eyes?
She was caught
without movement or sunlight
in a ritual unchanged for over 2,000 years.
Lacrimosa. Ah! What Weeping.

Surrounded by the heavy drip of candle
leaking wax to the guttered air;
by the pitched insistence of priests,
and incense crowding every corner
of that vaulted, belled chamber—
she was there! And received!

believed those faces in shawls
who were pointed in profile
as though quarried in stone from Lindos—
even if no one moved in wonder
at God's purpose working out.
For what else is faith, consoled her mother,

if not belief while being left behind—outside
all transfigurations within that box.
I know my child will soar
to where the unseen angels sing,
she sang. Kyrie Eleison.
Christi Eleison. Requiescat.

Dies Irae. Recordare.

On this day at the very edge of summer,
under a sky filling space
between distance and snow,
with the short switchgrass

and the mid and buffalo grasses
having become more—
thick grassland communities—
another child (also almost woman),

asks, which of us
is closer to Carolyn now, now
that she's gone to be with the stars?

I am where no circles are breaking

and rain falls on mountains
accepting fog,
as though they know
what will come tomorrow.

How can I tell if the letter I wrote
arrived before she died? Or does it sit,
still, on a front hall table collecting dust
and the discarded petals of too many flowers?

Did she know she was going;
that her mother was there
to watch a tumor take more and more to itself,
leaving less and less of a child?

Dies Irae. Why do comas take two weeks?
And where is that hole in the sky
they say is for spirit souls? Agnus Dei.
Miserere nobis. Dona nobis pacem.

Dies Irae. Tuba Mirum.

Hark the trumpet! sing anthems
to an earth where mourning stays lost
among the high plains. Be glad
you are where you are — atop prairies
resplendent with the profuse flowerings
of wild masses. What holds more wonder

than a color to sky
or rain's assuaging wetness;
than a day's sure turning
to its own volition —
the compass, its passing.

I have heard them chant,

"Somewhere the earth touches the sky
and the name of that place is the end."

You whom God left behind—gather strength
from unbroken circles
whether skies are cool
or the winds, sapphire.
Absorb this death, then spread her soul
among the grasslands:

the bluestems and gramas, the oats
and bamboo, the corns and sorghums.
God will repeat this day, forever,
so that we can weep
for one another, together.
Lux aeterna. Libera me. Requiescat.

IV

strike: *vb*, of a plant, to take root

root: *n*, the inner core or essential part of something

The Pink

When I lean across the river looking for snow;
When I am lean and carry stones across a river looking for snow;
When the fields say I told you,
having been harrowed to grow no more,
and it is March, and inattentive,
and the weeds hopelessly ocher;
When the porcelain lies fresh,
nervously incandescent with pearls
as though there were questions;
When there are frank hints that fall has come
but the bulls intervene, stampeding
each in front of the other in Jaipur;
When years of etching on rice paper
can lead only to stimuli in umbria Italia,
whereas divertisement among six patinated cabbages
hangs heavily in dishabille, or more to rose–red;
When in media res there can be no more accounting
of the things closest to God — What is this: Paradise?

Let the Ur landscapes begin! Let India order Brazil
out of the shipping lanes,
we are leaping towards Venezuela.
Allow the branches of some trees to grow old,
while all the while silence dries to tissue paper.
Hosanna! cries the child in her childlike manner
of descendents dressed in wisteria.
Let us not weep in front of the zinnias:
who will there be to address the hemlocks
escaping towards silver in the vaulted mountains.
Should there be color to sky after rain?
Let all glazes claim a clair de lune.

I wish to be old, fully embraced by capacity,
and named. I want to own a Great White Oak of Linnaeus.
Don't ask me for words only you possess,
lacquered and bright let daylight deliver them.
The eye must travel dimly, as only paintings under snow will.
Let us inherit pink, she said, the navy blue of India.

Cobb's Barns

Hopper painted this one empty of people.
From a ridge of dunes he saw
what someone else had built,
a set of barns attached
in the way a child's might be,
with each side seasoned a different
chromatic red—it being South Truro
and exposed, predictably,
to the permeability of air.
     "There are many thoughts,
     many impulses that go into
     a picture," Hopper once wrote,
     but he chose buildings not for beauty.

He caught the light that mattered
on the three planes
of the three roofs,
then provided solitude
where cows and other mud–bearing animals
are usually found. Hopper liked
the hills to look purple,
and he made the grasses common —
indigenous, they were given, therefore,
to a certain wildness.
A haze off the ocean is understood.
     "My aim," he told his wife,
     "is the most exact
     transcription possible."

By deed these barns belonged
to A.B. Cobb, unknown man,

until a painter's eye
in the summer of 1931
transferred ownership to himself,
and Cobb, in death, to immortality.
> (Look what) can be done
> with the homeliest subject
> if one possesses a seeing eye,
> they said of Hopper.

Did these giant forms filling their space
on sand like dinosaurian blocks,
fill an absence in Hopper as well?
> In the deliberate heat
> of a Cape Cod summer,
> as he divided the soil
> of his canvas with Cobb,
> Hopper allowed:
> "I don't know what my identity is."

Epithalamion

September 14, 1991
for K.D. and T. B.

Take it with you, this month. The days escape by the hour.

Grasses are greenest, a marsh, tallest. And a river, soon to be
    without its schooners,
glides gold; a glittering mirror to the noonday sun.

O Blue–Eyed Times! that barely change from generation.
Everything is lacquered yellow. Everywhere the bees are in full
    throttle.

Marry in September in Annisquam.
Who could want for more.

Yes, take these abbreviating days before they gain tomorrow.

Rain at night sweeps beaches clean, and a quiet claims the
    pasture —
it's possible to climb Squam Rock alone!

pure melodies you can hear
when after school children talk across Adams Hill Road,

and in the privet hedges insects drone along Leonard Street.

Did you know you'd marry as fall freshens Annisquam?
echo the halyards twanging off–shore rhythms to their tin–
    hollow masts.

From some ledge of memory September pulls us out,
    September bears away.

Yet we know, those of us who have had to leave it,
take it with you and it always brings you back.

Village of fishers argued from the Atlantic. Cape Ann hamlet
    cemented to rocks.

Inherit this New England shelf
then use its strengths to build your own.

Breathe in this bay of many blues, this autumn mix of low–tide
    life.

Out beyond the Old Wharf Lot, a kingfisher dives unheeded.
Atop Norwood Heights rose hips harden quickly.

These are the accustomed paths gleaned from our growing up,

where chains of clematis anchor asters to John Egan's land,
and a length of cove is flooded in birds.

Hold fast, September! To Annisquam.

Will you remember the colors of these houses,
the tomatoes that ripen on a Union Court porch?

Over all a lighthouse watches. Through it runs a river
concordant with the tides.

Marry now. It's September. In Annisquam.

Greed in Potter's Field

Two miles long, the Cabot Road cut–through
is a high ridge of access angling
like an unsheathed arrow between Cabot

in the Northeast Kingdom, and Lower Cabot,
home to the Creamery. The lookout

from this short cut is of the Creamery's
"backyard": fields and fields of farms stitched
in blanket seams to Mansfield's blue form — hazed

in the sunlit distance, but still there, for–
midable. Sun is everywhere on this late

September Sunday. The silos are silver
in it. Nichol's Pond shimmers
with it, and the unfurled Athyriums,

albeit jaundiced and actually curling
from last night's frost, clearly pretend

summer will last forever
alongside this embankment.
The only sign, in fact, of a season's

factual demise is in the pageant
overhead — signals of reds mantling

the maples that redden to wines then sugar
to clarets as though brewed in Bordeaux
instead of at home, here in Vermont — that

and the made–in–Vermont coon hanging
limp over the wired fence circling

Walther Bothfeld's cornfield. What got him (fence
nailed), beside greed? Was he shot and slung up
to rot, a farmer's guise of corning

belly–gods with cornfed greedyguts?
Or was it simply electrocution:

electrically arrested, then made
to wait—an object of transgression
out–flanked in front of Bothfeld's cows, for spring.

"A Morning View of Bluehill Village"

All he could see from this scene over Bluehill, Maine
(No distortions here. The work is from a seagirted light.),
is enough of a world for any man, it seems plain

from his painting dated 1824, September. Trailing a rain—
storm Fisher climbed up to get the angle right; to sight
all he could see from this scene over Bluehill, Maine—

distinctly no anthill: it looms more a mountain
at sea—as clarity would unveil, the view from this height
is enough of a world for any man. It seems plain

he set to as though knowing a sea captain
would pause 100 years later and hail: "How right!"
all he could see from this scene over Bluehill, Maine.

(Even now, gazing at houses piping like shanty refrains
down salted inlets, we are instilled with what, overnight
is enough of a world for any man.) It seems plain—

ly so American: three frocked figures in meadow of purslane;
a horse, a cemetery, stonewall; that our eye delights
all he could see from this scene over Bluehill, Maine
is enough of a world for any man, it seems plain.

The Day After Labor Day

On Lighthouse Beach a spaniel sat, his gladsome heart
in creaturely form, a metaphor for joy.
I'd watched him emerge from the water, assuming he'd soon
peel off—spring up through the pasture, then down
on into the village, for home. But the old tar
surprised me. Stretching to catch the sun's late
rays on his back, the tide's cool ebb
to a belly, the mariner addressed his command: *My God!*
it's glorious today (no people to interfere).
I'm where I want to be because I can be
(unlocked doors), and the well–seasoned, salt–fed,
"can't–let–a–day–go–by–without–a–swim"
sea dog continued to do just that—simply be there,
barking dull cares out the mouth of the river.

Who Knows the Mind of a Dog

Does she dream of heaven
as though nothing will change
after September? After the wrens
are through with their work;
the phlox, which drew her

into their curve, the radiance
of it, are spent — even after
rain sent in silk spinnakers
lets up — is there nothing more
except sleep? to dream
of a nearer sky, unafraid
it will be different there.
How huge a world it has become
since August. Time elongates,
filling in in right amounts
the buried seed for sorrow.

Who waits for whom?
Must I forget — forsaking
13 years of constancy
weighted down by dull routine —
what an awful consequence
silence is? Or will absence
be remembered? How far away
the mind of a dog lies.
We both know
she must go
to where I can't follow,
and who it is
who will decide, when.

Already it is closest to September
and the clethera bloom,
drawing the turtles out of the pond —
see them wild as hares!
while I am worn
by the murmurings
of insects at work. I hear
their elemental languages
forecasting angels.
Leaning into September,
a rhythmical breathing lifting
the daylight to its zenith hour,
the world empties itself of August
before the milkweed dries,
having an end before its time.

Strike Root

Strike root, my child,
while sparrows talk
on twilight wires
and pear trees bloom
in their own shafts
of natural light.

Come back to this rim
of opened window.
Here slatted lines,
bent by the height
of noon's shape,
admit a beautiful proportion.

My child don't be long. Otherwise
shallow roots spring up,
the kind that wither
in an August sun.
The damage will be there:
sorted by seed along stone wall.

Strike root, then, and take voice
to all the species; to those
living outside covenant;
to the ones left behind—we
who are separated
from ourselves.

A Killing Frost

We are the last in this cold air
to walk in the garden.
Ozone strikes at every corner,
to sting, hissing
at the summers of once–were,
bleaching them zinc white,
until what was permanent —
petals thick with dye,
with the gum and honey
from bees — dies back to dirt.

Other perspectives
might have been different.
The apple tree, leaning,
flames grenadine. The beeches
look ochre. What is left of the oaks
is chinese orange, while
the butterfly weed, called
cadmium yellow, is actually
orange. Unperturbed
the helianthus remain marigold.

These are flowers, believe me.
We know them by their impermanence
and a Herculean capacity to dye.
The cobalt platycodon grow where
the dog once walked. Last year
myosotis stained the hills
forget–me–not–blue. It was
a viridian Spring: Hemlocks rose

as though cypress, dyer's broom
bloomed among the acacia,

and no frost lapped
at the grass–green grass
until rain changed the series,
pouring grey into the ground,
into the dove grey fields
for the months ahead. Numbers
1, 2, 3 and 4—each a grizzled
square of pearls on paper—
when out–of–doors wear the bark
of ash trunks 200 years old.

Now the brief Prussian evening
is jet ink washing my lake pale
geraniums. In the lampblack
no one sees the batwings.
In the livid night they startle
no one with their weeping
that winter has set.
During this period, which
the radio calls seasonal,
many zinnias will die.

Anne Babson Carter was born in Gloucester, Massachusetts and graduated from Sweet Briar College in Virginia. She married D. Martin Carter M.D. in 1961. Together they raised a family while living in an eighteenth century center chimney house that sits beside a pond in Connecticut, and it is on this land that many of the poems in the book take place. Other poems are from journal entries kept by the poet while traveling with her husband, and from the fifteen years they lived in New York City. *Strike Root* is the winner of the 1996 Four Way Books Intro Series for first collections.